INSIDE TECHNOLOGY

INSIDE WEARABLE TECHNOLOGY

BY BRETT S. MARTIN

CONTENT CONSULTANT
Gwendolyn Hustvedt, PhD
Professor in Fashion Merchandising
Texas State University

Core Library
An Imprint of Abdo Publishing
abdobooks.com

Cover image: Wearable technology may someday include holographic images and menus.

abdocorelibrary.com

Published by Abdo Publishing, a division of ABDO, PO Box 398166, Minneapolis, Minnesota 55439. Copyright © 2019 by Abdo Consulting Group, Inc. International copyrights reserved in all countries. No part of this book may be reproduced in any form without written permission from the publisher. Core Library™ is a trademark and logo of Abdo Publishing.

Printed in the United States of America, North Mankato, Minnesota
092018
012019

Cover Photo: Dmytro Zinkevych/Shutterstock Images
Interior Photos: Dmytro Zinkevych/Shutterstock Images, 1; Twin Design/Shutterstock Images, 4–5; Featureflash Photo Agency/Shutterstock Images, 7; iStockphoto, 9; Kathy deWitt/Alamy, 10; Patrick T. Fallon/Bloomberg/Getty Images, 12; Andrej Sokolow/picture alliance/Getty Images, 14–15, 45; John Locher/AP Images, 19; Dmytro Zinkevych/iStockphoto, 21; Rawpixel/iStockphoto, 22; Kim Kyung-Hoon/Reuters/Newscom, 24–25; Shutterstock Images, 26, 32–33, 43; Arnold Gold/New Haven Register/AP Images, 35; Red Line Editorial, 36; Carlos Osorio/AP Images, 39

Editor: Megan Ellis
Series Designer: Ryan Gale

Library of Congress Control Number: 2018949750

Publisher's Cataloging-in-Publication Data

Names: Martin, Brett S., author.
Title: Inside wearable technology / by Brett S. Martin.
Description: Minneapolis, Minnesota : Abdo Publishing, 2019 | Series: Inside technology | Includes online resources and index.
Identifiers: ISBN 9781532117954 (lib. bdg.) | ISBN 9781641856201 (pbk) | ISBN 9781532170812 (ebook)
Subjects: LCSH: Technological innovations--Juvenile literature. | Wearable technology--Juvenile literature. | Smartwatches--Juvenile literature. | Virtual reality headsets--Juvenile literature.
Classification: DDC 621.381--dc23

CONTENTS

CHAPTER ONE
A Computer You Can Wear 4

CHAPTER TWO
Running on Hardware 14

CHAPTER THREE
Connecting with Software 24

CHAPTER FOUR
The Future of Wearables 32

Fast Facts 42

Stop and Think 44

Glossary 46

Online Resources 47

Learn More 47

Index 48

About the Author 48

CHAPTER
ONE

A COMPUTER YOU CAN WEAR

Mirah steps outside during her lunch break. She glances down at the device strapped around her wrist. It looks like a sleek watch, but it's much more. It's called a smart watch. Mirah presses the screen of the watch. Suddenly, it flashes to life. It displays the time. Then it tells her she's taken more than 8,000 steps since she woke up. Mirah has started a new fitness routine. She is halfway to her daily goal.

Mirah looks at the device again. She swipes left. The smart watch shows that her heart rate is in the normal range. Then the

The Apple Watch has many different apps. It can help people check messages and see incoming calls as well as tell the time.

SMART GLASSES

Designers and engineers are working on smart glasses that feel like regular glasses. Previous types of smart glasses have been too heavy. They have been hard to use. The technology company Intel has developed a new type of smart glasses called Vaunt. These glasses look like regular glasses. But they project a display onto the wearer's eyes. This display can show text messages, map directions, and incoming phone calls. The battery life is expected to be 18 hours for the smart elements. But the glasses will still help correct vision even when the battery runs out.

smart watch beeps. A text message appears. Mirah's friend Kayla wants to join her on her walk. Mirah smiles and sends a reply.

Mirah's smart watch is a piece of wearable technology. These devices are also known as wearables. Wearables are computers worn on the body. They are different from other electronics people could wear in the past such as pagers or CD players. Each wearable has sensors that collect data about the person wearing it. This helps people reach their goals for exercise, diets, and other activities.

Olympic gold medalist tennis player Bethanie Mattek-Sands wore Google Glass wearables to a party in 2013. Google Glass was discontinued for consumers in 2015.

GROWING RANGE OF PRODUCTS

In the 1960s, computers were very large. They took up entire rooms. In the 1980s, desktop computers became popular. For the first time, people owned personal computers. Laptop computers were invented in the 1980s. They became popular in the 1990s. Smartphones and tablets became popular in the 2010s.

Today, computers can fit inside wearable devices. The tiny computers collect and share data. Each type of device does a specific job. Tasks range from counting steps to checking blood pressure

EXTREME VIDEO CAMERAS

GoPro is a company that makes video cameras. These cameras are often used by people who do extreme sports. The cameras can be mounted on helmets. Many people use GoPro cameras to record activities such as sky diving and mountain biking. But GoPros have only been around since 2002. Before GoPros, people made custom wearables out of other technology.

In the 1980s, a mountain biker named Mark Schulz attached a video camera to his biking helmet. It recorded what he saw. The video he created is called "The Great Mountain Biking Video." The footage captures the intensity of the high-adrenaline sport.

WEARABLES ON THE BODY

As of 2018 there is a wearable for almost every part of the body. Look at the examples below. Why might these wearables work better on different parts of the body? How might people interact with their wearables?

Head
smart helmets and hats

Eyes
smart glasses and contact lenses

Ear
smart hearing aids

Body
smart patches, chips, and insulin pumps

Wrist
smart watches and fitness trackers

Legs and Feet
smart clothing and shoes

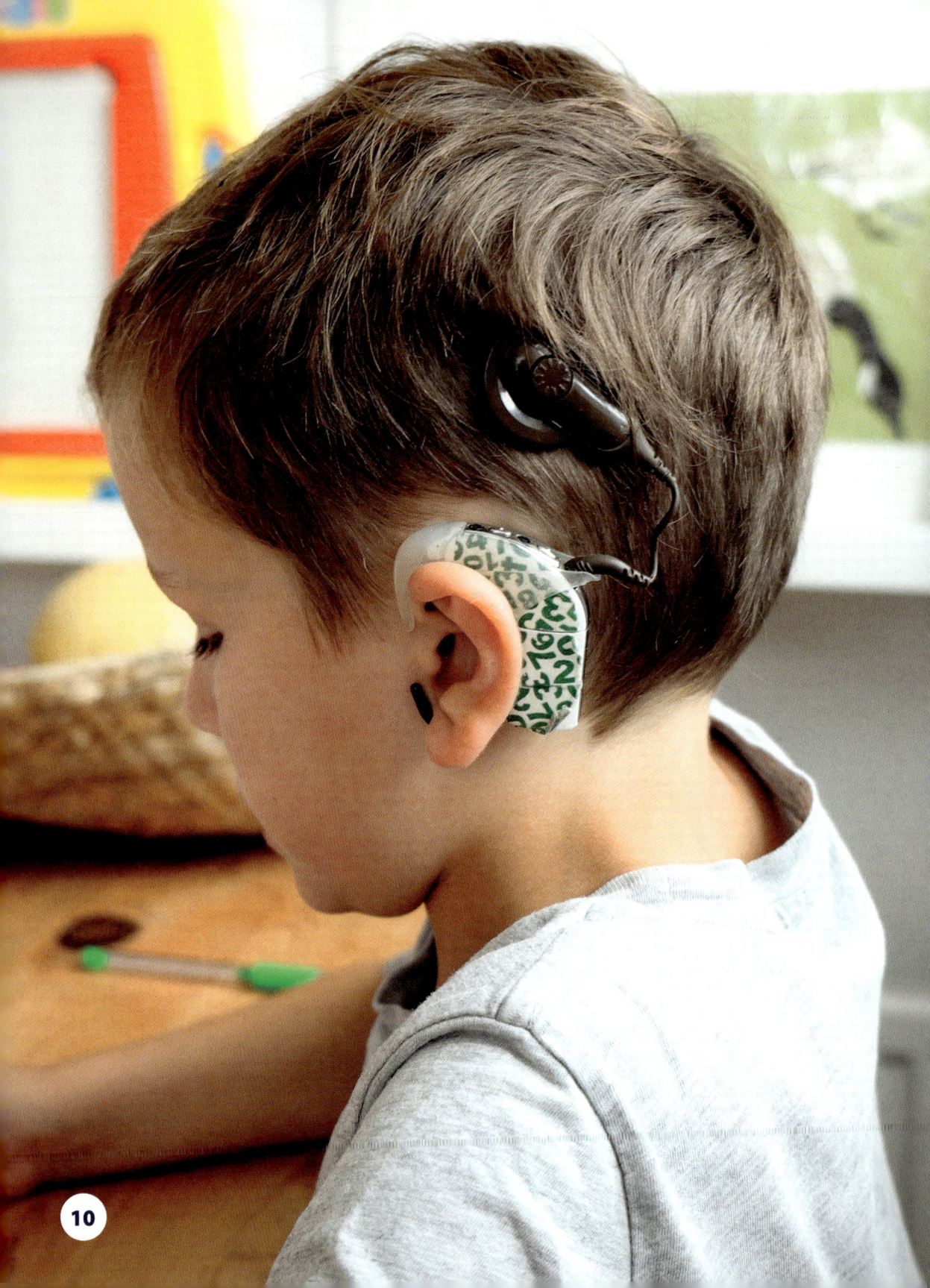

Some wearable devices are improvements on other types of technology, such as watches, insulin pumps, hearing aids, and pedometers. These devices did not used to have computers. But now they work better and faster. Other devices are in early stages of development, such as smart glasses that help people with directions or smart jewelry that can warn someone about a seizure, which is abnormal electrical activity in the brain.

Some wearable devices can connect users to the internet. They can show directions, play music, or answer questions. Wearers can check emails, answer texts, and take phone calls. Users can interact with them using touch screens or LED lights.

WHY WEAR TECHNOLOGY?

There are many reasons people use wearables. They may want to have their hands free to do other tasks. They may not want to manually synchronize, or update, information from a device to a computer. They may

A cochlear implant hearing aid uses processors and microchips to help people hear.

SNOW-1 smart bindings are wearables that attach to snowboards. They can analyze ride data and even record video.

want information immediately through haptic feedback. Haptic feedback uses slight vibrations to get the wearer's attention. The reminders may be to exercise, drink water, or meditate. This helps them stay healthy.

Some people want to understand how they spend their time. This makes them more aware of their daily actions. For example, some wearables show how well the user slept. Someone could use this data to improve sleeping habits.

Fitness trackers are a popular type of wearables. Some people want to see data about their workouts.

These wearables may also have health care apps. They may check blood sugar levels or heart rates. The apps may give users virtual awards and medals when they reach their goals. This turns wellness into a game.

Other wearables solve specific needs. Some wearables such as hearing aids and headphones help people hear. Wearables can send an alert if the wearer needs help. The devices offer real-time data. People can use the data to improve many aspects of their lives in ways never before possible. Wearable technologies can change how people live, eat, sleep, and exercise.

FURTHER EVIDENCE

Chapter One discusses wearable technology and covers different types of wearables available. What was one of the main points of this chapter? What evidence is included to support this point? Read the article at the website below. Does the information on the website support the main point of the chapter?

HOW SMART WATCHES WORK
abdocorelibrary.com/inside-wearable-technology

CHAPTER TWO

RUNNING ON HARDWARE

Wearables are available in many types of devices. Some of the most popular are wristbands, watches, jewelry, and glasses. Every type of wearable technology needs hardware. Hardware is the physical pieces that make wearable technology work. This includes screens and chips.

Wearables need hardware that is very small. It has to fit inside tiny spaces such as rings or watches. The form factor is very important. Form factor is the size, configuration, and arrangement of a wearable. It includes the internal components such as chips.

At the 2018 Mobile World Congress in Spain, Infineon showcased a chip that acted as a radar system.

SMALL SCREEN? NO PROBLEM

Most wearables have screens that display information. These screens are different sizes depending on the type of wearable. For example, the Fitbit Flex wristband has a very slim screen. It displays LED lights. These lights help users track their workouts. The Apple Watch has a more complex screen. It is the size of a typical watch face. It has an organic light-emitting diode (OLED) screen. This allows the watch to display sharp graphics in a wide range of colors.

SYSTEM ON A CHIP

Designing wearables is hard. People want them to have many features. Wearables need to connect to other pieces of technology. This requires advanced technology that fits in a tiny space.

New wearables use a system on a chip (SoC). It is a microchip. It includes electronic circuits. The circuits provide electricity to the wearable. The SoC powers wearables and other small devices such as smartphones. SoCs bring all the electronic parts onto an integrated circuit. An integrated circuit is a circuit that is built into the chip. Other parts on the circuit include a central processing unit (CPU) and data storage. The CPU controls the wearable. Storage holds different types of data. This data may include apps and other software. It may also include fitness information or text messages.

A SoC can have other hardware components too. These components include a modem for connecting to the internet. They also include memory to run apps and store software. Some SoCs can have a graphical processing unit, or GPU. This is what provides clear images on screens such as graphics on a smart watch.

> ### ARE SoCs REPLACING CPUs?
> People used to shop for computers based on the type of CPUs that computers had. The more CPUs, the more powerful the computer. Now people are buying devices based on the type of SoC. The tiny silicon chips are used in wearables, phones, and other devices. A single SoC can power an entire wearable. This gives it an advantage over CPUs, which cannot function without many other chips.

SENSOR POWER

Hardware supports sensors inside wearables. Sensors measure things. Some sensors in wearables include accelerometers, gyroscopes, and altimeters.

An accelerometer tracks movement. It's what counts how many steps a person takes. It can also tell which direction the wearable is facing. For example, some wearables change the orientation of the screen depending on which direction a person is holding it.

A gyroscope measures rotation and twist. It can measure a person's motions during a workout. It makes the data more precise than just the directions from an accelerometer.

An altimeter measures how high a person is above sea level or another point. It's helpful for a person who likes to climb mountains. Climbers can see exactly how high they are and plan routes to fit the altitude.

Other wearable sensors can measure electrolytes in sweat. They can also measure distance and speed.

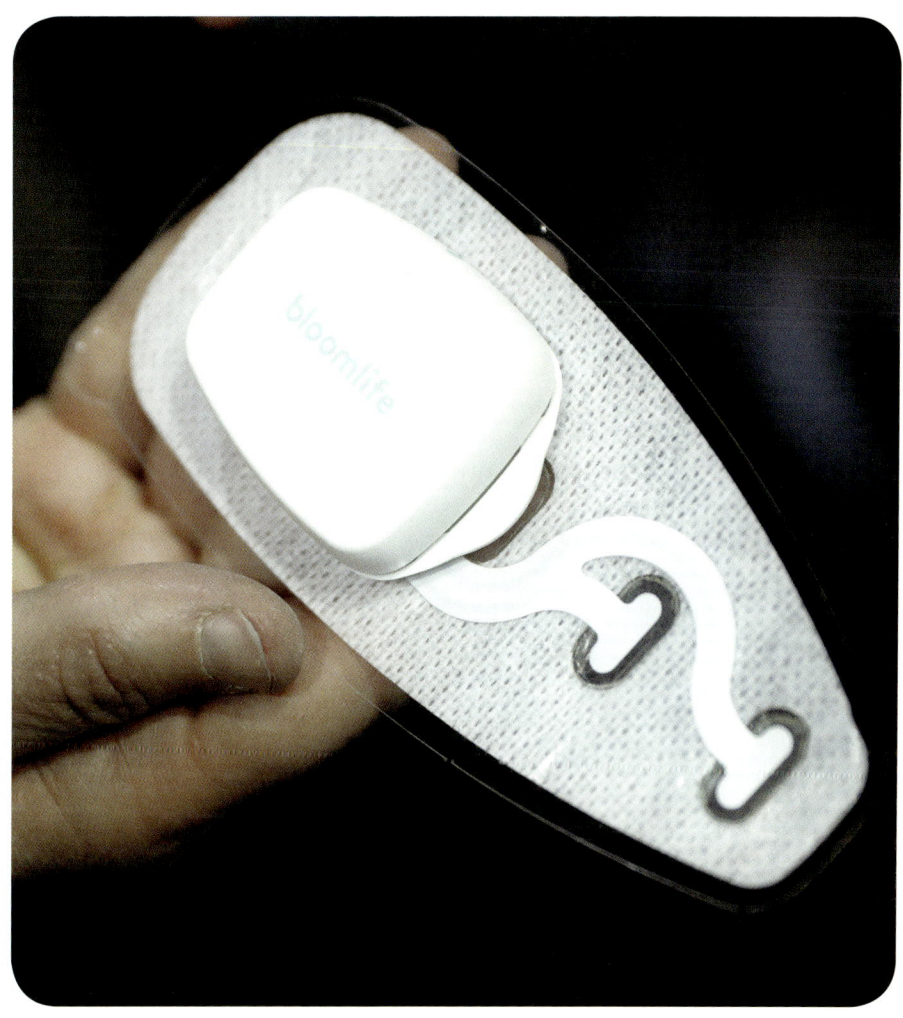

The Bloomlife wearable uses sensors to track and count contractions in people who are pregnant.

Sensors can work together to track movement in every direction. Algorithms turn data from the sensors into usable information, such as a person's body temperature.

COMMUNICATION

Wearables need to communicate with the internet or with other devices such as smartphones. Wires would make a wearable device hard to wear. The solution is wireless technology. This lets devices share data without being physically connected.

Bluetooth is one type of wireless technology. It has been available for consumer electronics since 2000. Bluetooth sends information using radio waves. It connects two devices together. Bluetooth receivers are ideal for wearables. The receivers are energy efficient and inexpensive. This helps save battery power. It also saves money.

Wi-Fi is another type of wireless technology. It also uses radio waves. But Wi-Fi signals go much farther than Bluetooth signals. Bluetooth is used to connect devices within 30 feet (9 m). Wi-Fi connects wearables

Some smartphones and wearables communicate with Near Field Communication (NFC). NFC connects wearables to devices that let people pay for items in stores.

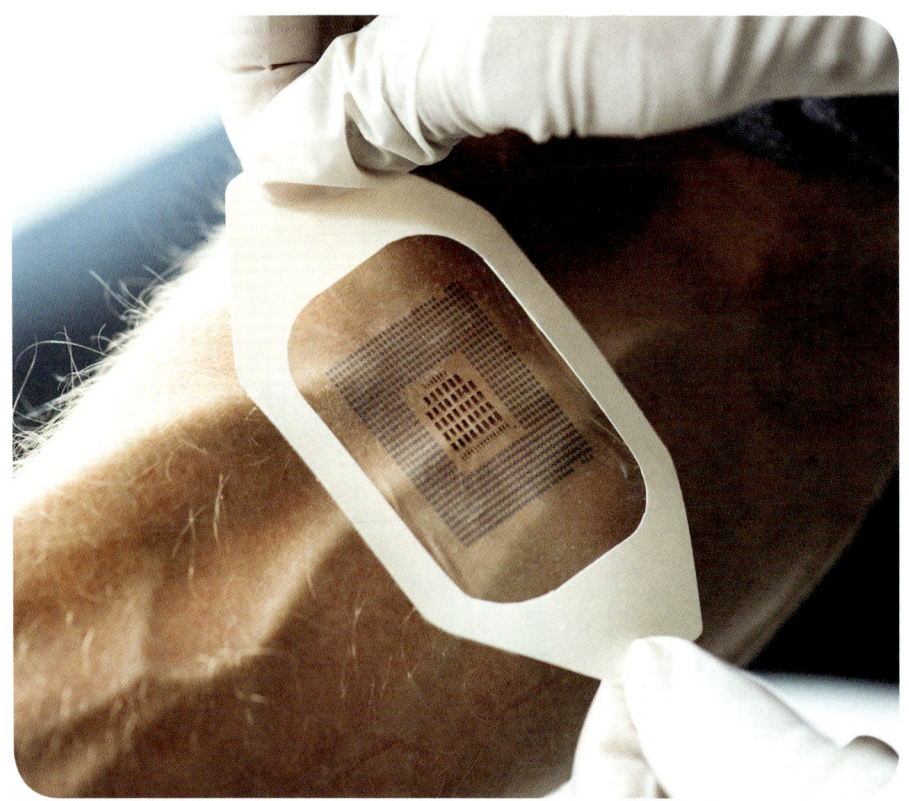

In the future, wearable technology may include implants or chips that can be scanned by other devices.

to the internet. These signals can be accessed up to 300 feet (90 m) away.

These wireless abilities allow wearables to easily share data. They also let wearables connect with the cloud and other people over the internet. This helps wearables send and receive messages, pictures, and other communications.

STRAIGHT TO THE SOURCE

One morning in 2015, Garry Barker put on his Apple Watch. It showed that his heartbeat spiked between 120 and 150 beats per minute. Barker went to the hospital. He was diagnosed with a blocked artery and an abnormal heartbeat. Barker credits the Apple Watch with saving his life. He says:

> Four sensors on the underside of the watch collect heart-rate information. . . . Two sensors are green and infrared LEDs. The other two are photodiodes [a device that turns light into electricity]. Blood is red because it reflects red light but absorbs green light. The watch uses its green LEDs paired with the light-sensitive photodiodes to detect blood flow through your wrist. . . . The LEDs . . . [allow] the watch to calculate your heart rate.
>
> Source: Garry Barker. "How My Apple Watch Saved My Life." *Sydney Morning Herald.* Fairfax Media, September 4, 2015. Web. Accessed July 24, 2018.

Back It Up

The author of this passage is using evidence to support a point. Write a paragraph describing the main point. Then write down two or three pieces of evidence the author uses to make the point.

CHAPTER THREE

CONNECTING WITH SOFTWARE

Hardware isn't the only thing wearables need. They also use software. Both hardware and software need to work together. All software uses at least one hardware device to work. The software is a set of instructions. It lets people interact with the wearable or perform tasks on it. For example, software is what allows the wearable to connect with the internet.

INTERNET OF THINGS

An internet browser is a type of software. The browser helps connect devices to the

A wearable for pets tracks their vital statistics. It connects to an app on the owner's smartphone and displays mood and overall health.

The IoT allows people to connect wearables to the internet. They can then access their files on the go.

World Wide Web. This is information such as websites and other resources that are accessed through the internet. Before, only computers could connect to the internet. But the Internet of Things (IoT) connects devices other than computers to the internet. These devices range from wearables to smartphones to home security systems. The IoT lets wearables share data with many other devices.

As more people buy wearables, more devices will be connected across the IoT. The IoT also connects devices to businesses. For example, doctors can connect to an app that a patient has on his wearable. This could help the doctor see vital statistics or specific information such as a person's blood pressure. This would save the patient time at the doctor's office.

OPERATING SYSTEMS

All wearables have an operating system (OS). The OS is a powerful type of software. It controls all of the hardware. It also controls other types of software. It opens and manages apps.

Several types of OSs are used in wearables. One popular system is Wear OS. It used to be called Android Wear. Wear OS lets Android smart watches perform tasks and connect people. Wearables using Wear OS listen for voice commands. Then they perform tasks.

The existence of the IoT means that there are many different types of wearables. Some have their own OS.

This can make it hard for wearables to communicate with each other. They might have different OSs.

AN APP FOR ALMOST ANYTHING

Thousands of apps are available for wearables. Apps are software that run on some devices. People download apps through app stores on the internet. These stores include the iTunes store and the Google Play store. Each app offers a unique feature or benefit. Apps can collect and store data. They can also keep people connected on social media.

Wearables and sensors can provide a lot of data just from touching someone's skin. Details can include heart rate, temperature, and muscle activity. An app then shows this data. It can also display movement, distance, and speed. These can help a person exercise safely.

Facebook and Twitter have apps designed for smart watches. People can check their messages or accept friend requests on the go. Another app called

WhatsApp shows messages on the wearable's screen. Wearers then reply with voice messages. More than 900 million people use this app on wearables or their phones.

However, not all wearables have apps. Some simple wearables such as pedometers only serve one purpose. They do not connect to the internet. They cannot download apps.

SOFTWARE IN THE CLOUD

People used to store their data on hard drives or discs. But the cloud offers a new way

MAP APPS

Technology that gives directions has been around since 1989. That's when the first Global Positioning System (GPS) device for consumers was released. Now, people can get directions and transportation information through apps. One free app is called Citymapper. It tells users the fastest route to get somewhere using transportation such as trains and buses. Users tell the app where they want to go. The app shows how long the trip would take. It also shows the cost of the trip. Additional features tell users the closest platform for a subway or the weather at the destination.

to save data. Data is stored in a system called the cloud. It is run by a company that offers data storage. There are many different cloud systems. The systems store the data in places called data centers.

The cloud lets several people use the data at once. This is helpful for people who connect to the IoT with several devices. If a wearable gets lost or stolen, the data is still in the cloud. This makes sure people always have access to their information. People often put music and pictures in the cloud. When they

DATA PRIVACY

One concern with wearables is how data in the cloud will be protected. Some people are worried about their privacy. They think their data might be stolen. A 2014 survey found that 86 percent of people worry about data security.

Security is a valid concern. Sometimes, app developers do not realize that data is visible to other people. This data can be stolen or hacked. In 2014, iCloud was hacked. It made headlines around the world. Personal pictures of celebrities were stolen. They were posted on the internet. This caused Apple to improve its cloud security.

want to play the songs or see the pictures, they access the cloud. All they have to do is connect to it through the internet.

Wearables often rely on cloud software. The software can be used in the cloud instead of being installed on wearables. This saves space on the wearable. It also helps with the life of the battery.

EXPLORE ONLINE

Chapter Three discusses cloud computing and storage. The website below discusses Nebula, a cloud computing platform created by NASA. As you know, every source is different. What information does the website give about how cloud computing helps NASA scientists? How is the information on cloud computing the same as the information in Chapter Three? What new information did you learn from the website?

NASA CLOUD COMPUTING PLATFORM: NEBULA
abdocorelibrary.com/inside-wearable-technology

CHAPTER FOUR

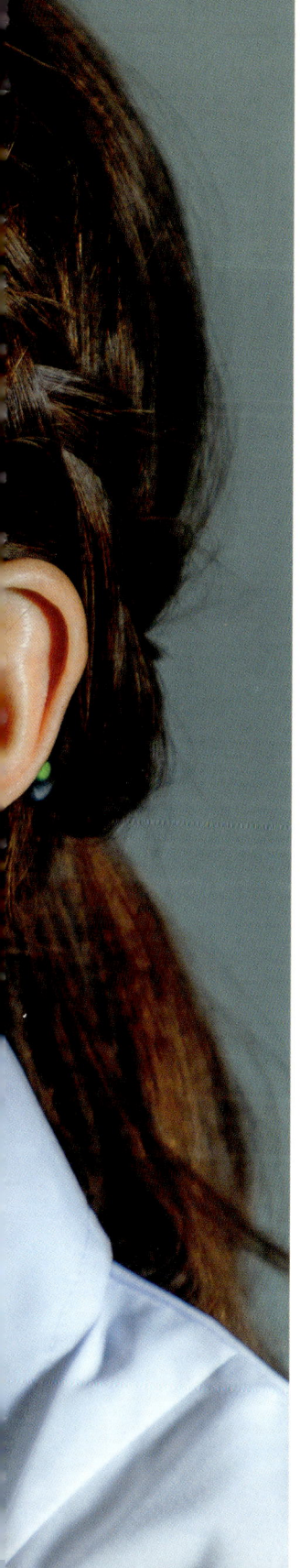

THE FUTURE OF WEARABLES

Wearable devices are expected to become even more popular in the future. Researchers predict that they will be the second best-selling consumer electronic device in the world. They also expect sales to grow 55 percent each year through 2020. In 2020, they predict that 305 million wearable devices will be sold.

NEXT-GENERATION HEALTH CARE

The health care industry is expected to see many benefits from wearables. Health care apps and wearables could get a boost from new microchips. For example, some

In the future, doctors may be able to use smart glasses to view scans or bloodwork from patients.

researchers are working on an artificial pancreas. It would monitor the level of sugar in a person's blood. It would then adjust a dose of insulin based on the data. This would be helpful for people with diabetes.

Researchers at the University of Virginia are working on a chip that provides real-time health monitoring. It uses body heat, motion, and sunlight as the energy source. The chip is being designed to detect changes in the body. For example, the chip might help a wearable tell the user that he is about to have an asthma attack.

Wearables in health care may even be placed inside the body. Microscopic computers could be inserted into tissues or blood vessels. They could provide the user with detailed health information. The device would gather data about potential problems.

The MiniMed 670G Insulin Pump System was approved by the FDA in 2016. This wearable automates how insulin enters the bloodstream.

HEALTH CARE WEARABLE SALES

Wearables are becoming very popular in health care. Experts predict that in 2021, global health care wearable sales will be approximately $17.8 billion. Look at the graph below. Why might people use wearables for health care? Why do you think sales are expected to double almost every year between 2018 and 2021?

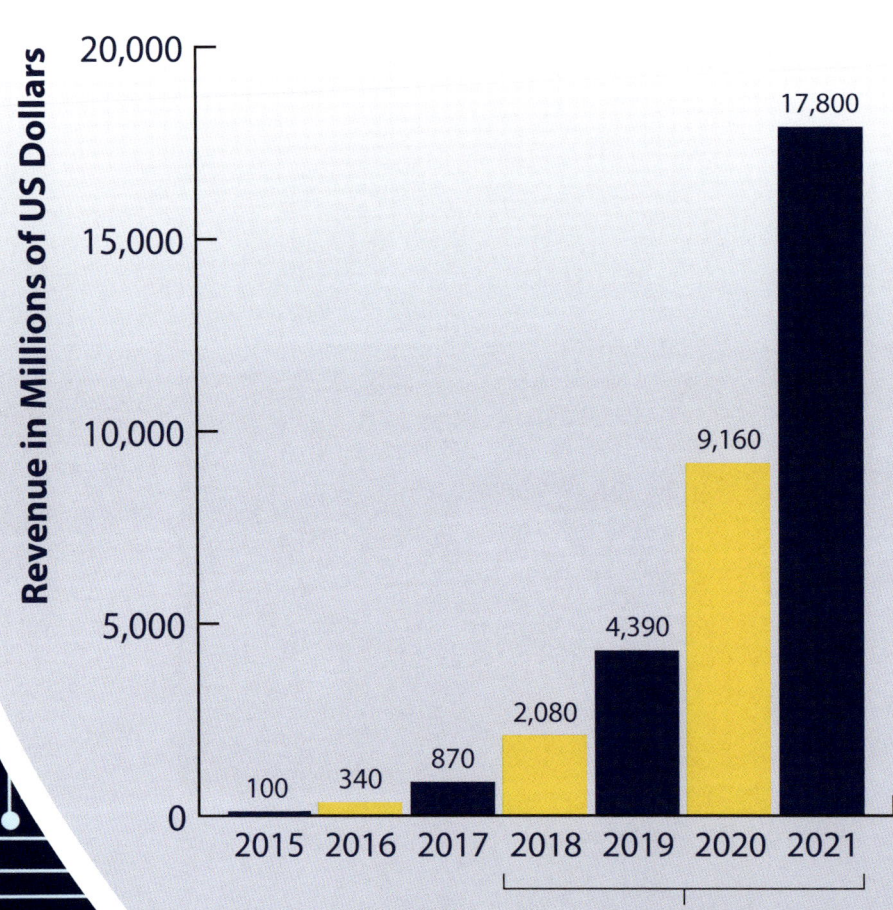

SMART CLOTHING

Technology and sensors are being woven into clothing. This is called smart clothing. Some analysts say smart clothes are the future of wearables. Like other wearables, smart clothing can provide haptic information. This might look like yoga pants with sensors and haptics. The sensors detect the relationship of the hips, knees, and ankles to see if the wearer has the correct posture. The haptics can then send vibrations at the hips, knees, and ankles. These tell the wearer how and when to move into the correct yoga positions.

DESIGNING A BETTER BATTERY

Batteries in wearables must be lightweight and small. Many wearables use lithium-ion batteries. These batteries are light. They also last for a long time. But people want batteries that can last even longer. The battery inside an Apple Watch lasts for 18 hours. Researchers are working on a battery that could last for 10 years on a single charge. This would change how people make wearables in the future.

Large sports and technology companies are entering the smart clothing market. These companies include Under Armour and Google. They want to make smart clothing as powerful as smartphones. The clothes would provide accurate data about the user.

WEARABLES AT WORK

Wearables can help people at work. For example, a wearable called the DAQRI Smart Helmet shows instructions on a visor. Workers can easily see them while having their hands free. Another wearable is a safety vest with a GPS inside. It tracks where employees are. First responders use these to stay safe. Other people know where they are even in dangerous situations.

In the future, wearables may be common in many workplaces. One company called Ekso Bionics creates bionic wearables as exoskeletons. They are used in some hospitals. They help people recover from accidents or strokes that leave them paralyzed.

The EksoVest is used at a Ford assembly plant in Wayne, Michigan. It helps assembly line workers avoid injuries when working on cars above their heads.

Ekso Bionics is branching out into other areas. It is creating wearables for people to use in factory and construction jobs. One wearable is the EksoVest.

It straps on like a regular vest. But it is spring-loaded. It helps people lift heavy things and avoid injuries.

Other companies may use wearables to help increase productivity and keep workers safe. Soon, there may be jobs that can only be done with wearable technology. As hardware and software are able to do more things, wearable technology will become part of everyday life for many people.

GETTING CHIPPED

In the future, some wearables may be implanted in the body. But before these products are available to consumers, they have to be tested. Some employees at Three Square Market, a tech company in River Falls, Wisconsin, are testing implants. They have radio frequency ID (RFID) microchips implanted in their hands. The chips are the size of a grain of rice. They help employees open doors and make phone calls. They even store documents and photos. Current uses of RFID implants are limited. However, these implants could make big changes in the future of transportation, health care, and banking.

STRAIGHT TO THE
SOURCE

Pankaj Kedia is the senior director of wearables at Qualcomm. In an interview with *Wareable*, Kedia discussed the difficulties of improving wearable hardware:

> [It's] designed from the ground up for a no-compromises smartwatch experience with dedicated chips that make your watch look pretty when you're not looking at it. . . . People have their normal watch where they can rely on long battery life, and then they have their smartwatch where the battery life is not as good and it does not look as sleek. . . . A smartwatch is first and foremost a watch . . . it needs to be sleek, it needs to look good when I'm looking at it or when I'm not looking at it. It cannot be static when I'm not looking at it; it cannot be black and white when I'm not looking at it.

Source: Hugh Langley. "Qualcomm's New Smartwatch Chips Launch Soon." *Wareable*. Wareable, May 8, 2018. Web. Accessed July 10, 2018.

Point of View
Kedia views fashionable smart watches as the future of wearables. What does Kedia say about how the new Qualcomm chip will answer current problems? Read back through this chapter. Do you agree? Why or why not?

FAST FACTS

- A wearable is a small computer that fits inside a device or clothing that's worn on the body.

- Computers used to be so big they filled an entire room. Now they're small enough to wear on a person's wrist.

- There are many types of wearables to fit specific needs.

- The form factor is the size, configuration, and arrangement of a computing device.

- A system on a chip, or SoC, is a microchip that fits inside wearables.

- Wireless technology lets wearables connect to other electronic devices and the internet.

- Sensors are placed inside wearables to measure motion, distance, and direction.

- Wearable devices record and share data about the people wearing them. Data can include steps taken in a day, amount of deep sleep in a night, or calories burned while exercising.

- The devices have a lot of health benefits. They encourage more exercise and better eating habits.

- Wearables range from digital hearing aids to smart glasses to smart clothing to smart watches.

- Hardware, software, and operating systems combine to make wearables work.

- The cloud provides a place to store wearable data.

- Data security is a big concern with wearables because the data can be hacked or combined with other data to reveal secrets.

- Some companies buy their employees wearables to make their jobs safer and easier.

STOP AND THINK

Say What?
Learning about wearable technology can mean learning a lot of new vocabulary. Find five words in this book you've never heard before. Use a dictionary to find out what they mean. Then write the meanings in your own words. Use each word in a new sentence.

You Are There
This book talks about the design and creation of wearable devices. Imagine you are creating a wearable device. What would you want it to be? How would it be different from what's already on the market?

Dig Deeper
After reading this book, what questions or concerns do you have about wearables? Look online for additional information on ways people and companies are using wearables. Write a paragraph about what you learned.

Another View

Chapter Three discusses cloud storage for data. As you know, every source is different. Ask a librarian or another adult to help you find another source about this topic. Write a short essay comparing the new source's point of view with that of this book's author. What is the point of view of each author? How are they similar and why? How are they different and why?

GLOSSARY

algorithms
sets of rules or procedures to solve a problem

central processing unit (CPU)
hardware that controls a computer

electrolytes
substances that help cells receive nutrients and get rid of waste products

exoskeletons
external skeletons that act as artificial supports

haptic
the use of vibrations for feedback in a device

microchip
a tiny wafer that has circuits on it

operating system (OS)
software that controls hardware and other software

pedometers
wearables that measure the distance a person traveled

sensors
devices that detect or measure something such as temperature or heart rate

system on a chip (SoC)
a microchip that combines many pieces of hardware on one chip

World Wide Web
a network of websites that are accessed through the internet

ONLINE RESOURCES

To learn more about wearable technology, visit our free resource websites below.

Visit **abdocorelibrary.com** for free Common Core resources for teachers and students, including vetted activities, multimedia, and booklinks, for deeper subject comprehension.

Visit **abdobooklinks.com** for free additional online weblinks for further learning. These links are routinely monitored and updated to provide the most current information available.

LEARN MORE

Kaul, Jennifer. *Inside Smartphones*. Minneapolis, MN: Abdo, 2019.

Kelly, James Floyd. *The Story of Coding*. New York: DK Publishing, 2017.

INDEX

accelerometer, 18
altimeter, 18
apps, 13, 17, 27–29, 30, 33

bionic wearables, 38–39
Bluetooth, 20

central processing unit (CPU), 17
cloud storage, 22, 29–31

Facebook, 28
fitness trackers, 9, 12–13

graphical processing unit (GPU), 17
gyroscope, 18

haptic feedback, 12, 37
hardware, 15–19, 25, 27, 40, 41
hearing aids, 9, 11, 13

insulin pumps, 9, 11, 34
internet browsers, 25–26
Internet of Things (IoT), 26–27, 30

laptop computers, 8

microchips, 15–16, 33–34, 40

operating system (OS), 27–28, 31

pedometers, 11, 29

smart clothing, 9, 37–38
smart glasses, 6, 9, 11, 15
smart watch, 5–6, 9, 11, 13, 15, 16, 17, 23, 27, 28, 37, 41
smartphones, 8, 16, 20, 26, 38
software, 17, 25–31, 40
system on a chip (SoC), 16–17

tablets, 8
Twitter, 28

Whatsapp, 29
Wi-Fi, 20–22

About the Author

Brett S. Martin has more than 20 years of writing experience. He has worked as a reporter, editor, director of public relations, and president of his own media company. He has written several fiction and nonfiction books. Martin lives in Shakopee, Minnesota, with his wife and two teenage sons.